GOD,
I Need Your Comfort

KAY ARTHUR

HARVEST HOUSE PUBLISHERS

EUGENE, OREGON

All Scripture quotations are taken from the New American Standard Bible®, © 1960, 1962, 1963, 1968, 1971, 1972, 1973, 1975, 1977, 1995 by The Lockman Foundation. Used by permission. (www.Lockman.org)

Cover by *Koechel Peterson & Associates, Inc., Minneapolis, Minnesota*

Select quotations from *A Shepherd Looks at Psalm 23* by W. Phillip Keller. Copyright © 1970 by W. Phillip Keller. Used by permission of The Zondervan Corporation.

GOD, I NEED YOUR COMFORT

Copyright © 1991 by Kay Arthur
Formerly titled *Because the Lord Is My Shepherd*
Published by Harvest House Publishers
Eugene, Oregon 97402
www.harvesthousepublishers.com

Library of Congress Cataloging-in-Publication Data

Arthur, Kay, 1933–
  God, I need your comfort / Kay Arthur.
    p. cm.
  ISBN 0-7369-1228-2 (pbk.)
  1. Consolation. I. Title.
  BV4905.3.A78 2004
  242'.4—dc22   2004004800

Printed in the United States of America

04 05 06 07 08 09 10 11 12 / VP-KB / 10 9 8 7 6 5 4 3 2

Contents

Psalm 23
A Psalm of David

⌣

The LORD is my shepherd, I shall not want.
He makes me lie down in green pastures;
He leads me beside quiet waters.
He restores my soul; He guides me in the paths of
righteousness for His name's sake.
Even though I walk through the valley of the
shadow of death, I fear no evil, for You are with me;
Your rod and Your staff, they comfort me.
You prepare a table before me in the presence of my
enemies; You have anointed my head with oil;
my cup overflows. Surely goodness and
lovingkindness will follow me all the days of my life,
and I will dwell in the house of the LORD forever.

A Psalm for You

Do you ever get lonely, my friend? I do. I think everyone gets lonely sometimes, and for each of us, loneliness is triggered by something different, something personal.

As I sit down to write this, I am all alone...and I feel a little weepy. I wish Jack were home, but he is away. In a few days I will be joining him, and for several weeks we will minister together. Our days will be occupied with people and service—and we will experience fulfillment. And yet I know the loneliness will come back. I won't want it to, but something will trigger a thought, and once again I'll have to deal with it.

How? I will remember the truths of Psalm 23, and there I will find the precepts, which—though they do

Lord is my shepherd, I shall not want. He makes me lie down in green pastures; He leads me

6 of Kay Arthur

not remove the loneliness and the pain—enable me to live.

The words are so familiar: "The LORD is my shepherd, I shall not want" (Psalm 23:1). Familiar...like seeing an old friend...because we have heard them over and over again.

Maybe you memorized them in Sunday school. Maybe the words seem like an old friend because Psalm 23 is often read at funerals. Maybe the familiar words brought you comfort and assuaged your fear of death: "Even though I walk through the valley of the shadow of death, I fear no evil, for You are with me."

When you heard Psalm 23 as a child, you learned that God would always be with you. When you hear it as an adult, you are reminded that even in death God will be there. But meanwhile, what does one do for the day-by-day experiences which are bound to bring loneliness, apprehension, and anxiety?

The same psalm memorized in childhood and heard in the hour of death has the answers, for each day has enough trouble of its own (Matthew 6:34).

Psalm 23 is not merely a charming allegory for children or a memorial for the dead. It is a psalm for living. It is a psalm of comfort for life, no matter what life brings, and its truths are summed up in the first and glorious verse: "The LORD is my shepherd, I shall not want."

It is a psalm for the 40-year-old man whose letter broke my heart when he told me, for the first time, what his parents had done to him when he was a child. When he was only 9 years old, he had walked into his parents' room one day while they were looking at child pornography. As I read what they had done to him, I groaned in sorrow. His words came haltingly, even on paper. Some words were missing, replaced with dashes, for they were too perverted, too obscene, too twisted even to be written down. His parents did to him what they saw on the videotapes and in the magazines…and it went on for three years until, at age 12, he finally ran away. He ran away from the perversion, but he could not escape the anguish of memories which had become ever more frequent.

It is a psalm for a friend, younger than I, who has a brain tumor.

It is a psalm for another friend who seeks to live moment-by-moment above the rejection of her family, the weariness of earning a living, and the loneliness of her singleness.

Even though I walk through the valley of the shadow of death, I fear no evil, for You are with

It is a psalm of promise for my brothers and sisters who once lived under the atheistic tyranny of communism and to whom we now minister as they seek to know their Shepherd even better.

It is my psalm of assurance. When my days come to an end, I will turn around and see that even the small pain I experienced and the great pain my friends experienced will be seen as "goodness and lovingkindness."

I know the words may be familiar, but read them again…thoughtfully. Watch how the pronoun referring to the Lord changes from "He" to "You" in verse 4.

Now, read it once again—this time aloud. Did you notice what the Shepherd does for His sheep and the benefits which come to the sheep as a result of the Shepherd's care?

And, what does the sheep have to do? Selah—pause and think on it.

Is this a psalm for you, Beloved?

me; Your rod and Your staff, they comfort me. You prepare a table before me in the presenc

Your Great Need for a Shepherd

*I*f you are ever going to know the Shepherd's care, you must first realize your great need for a shepherd. And I truly believe that God created sheep so that we could see that need…to see what we are like. For if any animal ever needed a shepherd, it is sheep!

Sheep are helpless, timid, feeble creatures that have little means of self-defense. They are among the dumbest of all animals, and because of this they require constant attention and meticulous care. If sheep do not have the constant care of a shepherd, they will go the wrong way, unaware of the dangers at hand. They have been known to nibble themselves right off a mountainside! They will overgraze the same land and run out of food unless the shepherd

enemies; You have anointed my head with oil; my cup overflows. Surely goodness and

leads them to new pastures, and if they are not led to proper pastures, they will obliviously eat or drink things that are disastrous to them.

Sheep easily fall prey to predators, and when they do, they are virtually defenseless. Sheep can also become cast down and, in that state, panic and die. And so, because sheep are sheep, they need shepherds to protect and care for them.

If you belong to the Lord, you, Beloved, are the sheep of His pasture. It was for you that God brought up from the dead the great Shepherd of the sheep through the blood of the eternal covenant, even Jesus our Lord (Hebrews 13:20). Jesus is there for you, and because He is, although your life might be difficult or fraught with testings, you shall not want. This is His promise.

The question then becomes, where do you turn? To whom do you run?

Hebrews 7:24,25 says: "But Jesus, on the other hand, because He continues forever, holds His priesthood permanently. Therefore He is able also to save forever those who draw near to God through Him, since He always lives to make intercession for them."

Your Good Shepherd is there at the right hand of the Father. He lives within… "Christ in you, the hope of glory" (Colossians 1:27). He holds you in His hand and…underneath are the everlasting arms.

O precious sheep, don't run to the arms of flesh when you're being held in the arms of El Olam, the everlasting God. He's *your* shepherd. You shall not want.

⟿

The Shepherd sought His sheep,
The Father sought His child;
They followed me o'er vale and hill,
O'er deserts waste and wild;
They found me nigh to death,
Famished and faint and lone;
They bound me with the bands of love,
They saved the wand'ring one.

—HORATIUS BONAR

Lord is my shepherd, I shall not want. He makes me lie down in green pastures; He leads me

beside quiet waters. He restores my soul; He guides me in the paths of righteousness for His nar

Your Shepherd...
All-Sufficient

The welfare of sheep depends solely upon the care they get from their shepherd. The better the shepherd, the healthier the sheep. When you see weak, sickly, or pest-infested sheep, you can be sure that their shepherd really does not care well for them.

What is our Great Shepherd like? Learn that, and you will understand why you can confidently say, "The Lord is my shepherd, I shall not want." Believe it, and you will know a life of perfect rest.

Psalm 23, which shows us the ministry of our *Great* Shepherd, is surrounded by two psalms that show us two other aspects of our Shepherd. Psalm 22 shows us the *Good* Shepherd, who lays down His life for His sheep, and Psalm 24 shows us our *Chief* Shepherd, the King of Glory, who is to come again (1 Peter 5:4).

Even though I walk through the valley of the shadow of death, I fear no evil, for You are with

Before the Lord can ever function as your Great Shepherd, however, you must first know Him as your Good Shepherd, because it is here that you meet Him as your precious Savior. Listen to His words: "Truly, truly, I say to you, I am the door of the sheep" (John 10:7).

There is no other door, there is no other way to enter in and become God's sheep, except by Jesus: "All who came before Me are thieves and robbers, but the sheep did not hear them" (John 10:8).

His sheep hear His voice; that is, they know truth when they hear it. And once they hear truth, they recognize it for what it is—reality!

Jesus said, "I am the door; if anyone enters through Me, he will be saved [perfect security], and will go in and out [perfect liberty] and find pasture [perfect sustenance]" (John 10:9).

A shepherd who knew nothing of God's Word was describing his sheepfold to a curious inquirer. As he pointed to the sheepfold, the inquirer said, "But where is the door?"

"I am the door," the shepherd replied. "At night, when the sheep enter the sheepfold, I lie down in the opening. Nothing can enter or leave without going over me, because I am the door."

Have you heard His voice? Have you entered into the sheepfold of God's forever family through Jesus the Christ? If so, then you're secure and beloved of God. Nothing can ever come into your life without His knowledge and permission. And if it does come—it will be for your good and His glory (Romans 8:28-39).

∼

Good Shepherd
Great Shepherd
Chief Shepherd

enemies; You have anointed my head with oil; my cup overflows. Surely goodness and

...ovingkindness will follow me all the days of my life, and I will dwell in the house of the Lord fore...

You Shall Not Want

*H*e walked into a nine-foot cell and was immediately imprisoned in darkness. As the bolt slid smoothly across the bars and the padlock was fastened on the door, he found himself caught in a night of steel, bound in bands of iron. It was October 1950. Geoffrey Bull was a prisoner in China.

"I had no Bible in my hand, no watch on my wrist, no pencil or paper in my pocket. There was no real hope of release. There was no real hope of life. There was no real possibility of reunion with those I loved. The only reality was my Lord and Savior Jesus Christ. Divested of all, He was to become everything to me. He was to break my bars and enlarge my coasts in the narrow room. He was to be my fullest nourishment amidst the meager food. My meat which my captors 'knew not

Lord is my shepherd, I shall not want. He makes me lie down in green pastures; He leads me

of.' He would make me glad with His countenance. He would let me hear His voice. As in the days of His nativity, Herod may reign and imagine slaughter against the innocent, but let me only see His star and I would come to worship Him."[1]

What if that had been you instead, Beloved, imprisoned in that cell? Would you know your Shepherd well enough to be able to say in confident faith, "The Lord is my Shepherd, I shall not want"? In the darkness of the night of imprisonment would you know enough to look for His star so that you might worship Him?

Or maybe I should say, in your prison—whatever the bars are made of—have you looked beyond to the One who is above, beneath, and within? Are you worshiping Him?

What does it take to be able to worship God and confidently proclaim Him as your all-sufficient Shepherd? Worship is based on knowledge...a knowledge that I pray will be wonderfully deepened as we explore this psalm together. To worship God is to recognize His worth and to bow before Him.

Suppose someone were to ask you, "What is your Shepherd like that He could so provide for you that you would not want...no matter what...even if you found yourself in a prison cell?"

How would you answer, Beloved?

When Moses met God at the burning bush, God commissioned Moses to stand before Pharaoh and say, "God says, 'Let My people go, that they may serve Me.'" Moses responded by asking, "Who am I, that I should go to Pharaoh, and that I should bring the sons of Israel out of Egypt?" (Exodus 3:11). Interestingly enough, God never answers Moses' question about his personal qualifications for such a task. Rather, we find God saying to him, "Certainly I will be with you" (Exodus 3:12). Moses would not want; the Shepherd was his for the task. All Moses had to do was follow.

However, to do this, Moses did need to know who his God was. He needed to know who was going to separate the children of Israel out of Pharaoh's sheepfold. So Moses asked God His name. "Who shall I say sent me?" Oh, how I love God's answer: "I AM WHO I AM....Thus you shall say to the sons of Israel, 'I AM has sent me to you.'...This is My name forever, and this is My memorial-name to all generations" (Exodus 3:14,15).

Even though I walk through the valley of the shadow of death, I fear no evil, for You are with

I AM! I AM what? I AM all you will ever need. I AM all you will ever need at any time, in any place, in any situation.

O Beloved, our Shepherd is our El Shaddai. Some schools believe this name for God, El Shaddai, comes from the word "breast"—the place for succoring one's child. God is our All-Sufficient One, whose grace is sufficient for us so that we can be "content with weaknesses, with insults, with distresses, with persecutions, with difficulties, for Christ's sake; for when I am weak, then I am strong" (2 Corinthians 12:10).

What has God asked you to do? Where has your Shepherd led you? Does it seem too hard? Too difficult? Impossible because of who you are?

O Beloved, look to your Shepherd! You shall not want, for He is your El Shaddai, your "I AM." He is all you will ever need. That is His memorial-name forever, even to you, to your generation.

Your Shepherd is the Sovereign God. "His sovereignty rules over all" (Psalm 103:19).

"His dominion is an everlasting dominion, and His kingdom endures from generation to generation. All the inhabitants of the earth are accounted as nothing, but He does according to His will in the host of heaven and among the inhabitants of the earth; and no one can ward off His hand or say to Him, 'What have You done?'" (Daniel 4:34,35).

If you are going to live a life of peace, a life of rest and contentment no matter what your circumstances, you must be aware of the sovereignty of your Shepherd. When you entered into the sheepfold, you saw that the One who laid down His life for you was truly God incarnate, God in the flesh. Now you must know that, as God, your Shepherd is sovereign. To recognize His sovereignty is to worship Him aright.

When we say that God is sovereign, we mean that nothing can happen in this universe without God's permission. Oh, man retains his free will and responsibility, but they cannot be executed unless God concurs. Neither necessity, nor chance, nor malice of Satan controls the sequence of events or their causes. God is the supreme Ruler over all, and no one nor any circumstance of life can thwart His desire or His plan. Your Shepherd is the sovereign Ruler of all the universe, Beloved, and that is why you shall not want.

Why don't you take a few minutes and meditate upon this truth? You may want to write out exactly what God's sovereignty means to you, listing the particular things in your life over which God has control.

enemies. You have anointed my head with oil; my cup overflows. Surely goodness and

...lovingkindness will follow me all the days of my life, and I will dwell in the house of the Lord fore...

Your Shepherd Loves You

The baby was choking. Frantic with fear, the young mother picked her up and ran to the car. She had to get to the hospital. Hurriedly she backed out of the garage, not noticing that her older daughter was playing in the driveway. She ran over her and killed her.

As this beautiful young mother shared her story with me, my heart wrenched with the horror of it all. I thought, "O Father, how could she handle it if she did not understand Your sovereignty?" But she did know the sovereignty of God.

What had happened was horrible. It was painful. But it did not destroy her. She was not a demented soul locked in a padded cell of what ifs, whys, and if onlys. She did not bitterly harangue God, asking Him why He had permitted this. Nor did she refuse the open arms that drew her to her El Shaddai and His all-sufficient breast. And I, along with others, saw her peace and realized once again what it means to have the Lord as our Shepherd.

When I have a difficult time understanding how a sovereign God can permit all the pain and suffering that permeates and invades every level of our society, I have to turn and run to what I know of His character. And the first place I run is into my knowledge of the fact that God is love.

The One who sits upon His throne ruling over all the universe is a God of love (1 John 4:8). Love is the very essence of His being; He can never act apart from love. He loves us with an everlasting love, a love that will not fail, a love that continually seeks our highest good.

His sheep are in His hands, and those hands are hands of love. Nothing…not any situation nor any person…can snatch us out of His hands.

Listen to His words: "My sheep hear My voice, and I know them, and they follow Me; and I give eternal life to them, and they will never perish; and no one will snatch them out of My hand" (John 10:27,28).

Your Alpha and Omega

Have you ever felt caught or trapped in a situation that seems absolutely insane, horrid, unbelievable, inconceivable? All of a sudden your plans, dreams, hopes are shattered.

It's like a nightmare. *This can't be happening to me*, you think. *It will alter the course of my life. It will ruin everything!* You wonder how you'll survive. Gloom settles like a fog over your heart and mind, and dire forecasts of danger loom through the night of your imagination.

Suddenly you panic. What should you do? You have to do something…but what?

The clap of thunder causes the little sheep to stop his grazing and look up. The sudden noise and the pelting of the rain have his attention. Panic sets in. Where is his shepherd?

Even though I walk through the valley of the shadow of death, I fear no evil, for You are with

Fear not, little flock…your Shepherd is watching over you.

"Remember this, and be assured; recall it to mind…for I am God, and there is no other; I am God, and there is no one like Me, declaring the end from the beginning, and from ancient times things which have not been done, saying, 'My purpose will be established, and I will accomplish all My good pleasure'…Truly I have spoken; truly I will bring it to pass. I have planned it, surely I will do it" (Isaiah 46:8-11).

O beloved sheep, whatever happens, you can know that His will shall be accomplished in your life…because you are His. He is the Alpha and the Omega, the Beginning and the End. Your Shepherd has not left you; He is there to complete that which He has begun—to make you into His image. His plan for you will not be thwarted. All that God inaugurates, He completes. He is the God of the finished work.

So rest, little sheep, your Shepherd is there. He is in control. Whatever comes to you has been filtered through His fingers of love, and it will serve to accomplish His purpose.

me; Your rod and Your staff, they comfort me. You prepare a table before me in the presence

Your Times...in His Hands

ave you ever become frustrated because suddenly you have been held up or kept from carrying out your plans? Have you become agitated, impatient, angry?

O little sheep, why do you get all upset? The Shepherd is there. Did He not lead you this far? The steps of a man are established by the Lord (Psalm 37:23). "Man's steps are ordained by the LORD; how then can man understand his way?" (Proverbs 20:24).

You do not need to understand. Quit your frustration. Walk by faith, knowing that goodness and mercy are following you because the Lord is your Shepherd. Your times are in His hands (Psalm 31:15).

The eternal God is the Author of time, and every moment counts to Him. He will not squander your

enemies; You have anointed my head with oil; my cup overflows. Surely goodness and

time. He has a precious blessing…a precious lesson for you at every turn. Rest and "in everything give thanks; for this is God's will for you"…otherwise it could not happen.

A pastor was headed for a speaking engagement across the country. He rushed through the airport to make his connection, only to find that the plane was to be delayed for at least an hour. The pastor's smile was refreshing to the airline agent, quite unlike the angry complaints he had been receiving from other irate travelers. The pastor simply said, "My times are in God's hands, so I don't sweat it!"

With an hour to spare and a promise that they would not leave without him, the pastor went to eat. Fifty minutes later when the pastor returned, the agent turned ashen.

"You got on the plane ten minutes ago. I saw you. How could you be standing here?"

The pastor smiled. "Obviously that wasn't me. I'm here."

Now a deathly white, the agent said, "But I saw you. I know it was you. I saw your ticket and boarding pass."

The pastor just shook his head. "But I'm here."

Later the news came. The plane had crashed. All were killed.

Your times are in the hands of the sovereign God, dear sheep, so do not fret. Rest. If God makes you stand and wait, see it as gain, not loss. It all has a purpose…His.

Have you ever wondered, Where is this life of peace that is supposed to belong to the child of God? Do you ever toss and turn because your mind will not allow your body to rest? Pressures, fears, unhappy relationships tramp up and down the corridors of your mind, forbidding sleep. The night grows long; you grow weary…and in your weariness you wonder if this is all there is.

No, Beloved…not if the Lord is your Shepherd. He will make you lie down in green pastures (Psalm 23:2). This is the Great Shepherd's promise to His sheep…a promise of rest.

Why, then, is there no rest? Why? Because, Beloved, in some way you have failed to appropriate the grace of God, which He says is sufficient for all of your needs (2 Corinthians 12:9). For sheep, true rest is to lie down in green pastures. But before they can do that, they must be free from four things. Phillip

Keller introduces these keys to rest in his excellent book, *A Shepherd Looks at Psalm 23*. I want to make you aware of what these four things are, and then we will take them one by one and discuss them in a practical way. So follow closely, precious sheep, as we pasture at Psalm 23:2 for a while, gleaning all that we can.

First, sheep must be free from hunger. They cannot lie down as long as they are hungry. Yet, in this second verse of the Twenty-third Psalm we find that the Shepherd has so satisfied the sheep's hunger that they can lie down right in the midst of green pastures.

Second, if sheep are to rest, they must be free from fear. Are you, Beloved, beset with fears? Is it no wonder you toss and turn?

Third, sheep cannot rest unless they are free from friction. Tension with others of their kind keeps them on their feet…they feel they must defend themselves!

And fourth, sheep cannot rest unless they are free from pests. Sheep can be greatly aggravated, even driven to distraction, by flies, parasites, or other pests that seek to torment them.[2]

Which of these things holds you prisoner? What hungers, what fears, what frictions, what aggravations?

Food That Satisfies

Hours are spent in our ministry, not only in teaching but in listening...weeping... praying...and then instructing.

Often we shake our heads in disbelief—not that we think what we are hearing is a lie; rather, in disbelief that people should suffer such trauma at the hands of others or get themselves into such painful predicaments.

Oh, the awful, awful wages of sin! Self-inflicted or afflicted! Have you ever wondered how people get so messed up? Or why are they so restless...so tormented ...so anxious about life? It's because they do not intimately know the Shepherd of the sheep. Or, having known Him, they have refused to follow Him.

They have not known nor fed upon the green pastures of His Word. And because of hunger they have

Even though I walk through the valley of the shadow of death, I fear no evil, for You are with

been constantly foraging for something to satisfy their inner craving.

Sheep that are hungry won't lie down. They can't. They lack vigor and vitality, and yet they are driven because they are not satisfied. So, untended by the shepherd, they eat anything and everything, ofttimes to their own destruction.

This is what has happened to so many people with whom we have shared. They have not fed upon the Word of God; they have not desired the sincere milk of the Word that they might grow thereby (1 Peter 2:2). Nor have they gone on to strong meat that they might be mature in the faith, able to discern good and evil doctrine (Hebrews 5:14).

O Beloved, what has hunger caused you to do? Where has it led you? Will you not allow your Shepherd to lead you to green pastures where He might nourish you in His Word? This is the passion of my life, His call—to teach people how to feed on His Word, to discover truth for themselves through our varied inductive studies. Your hunger for more can be satisfied.

me; Your rod and Your staff, they comfort me. You prepare a table before me in the presenc

His Pastures...
His Word

The Lord has told me I must talk with you. When can we get together?" Oh, how I admired this chaplain. Pride would not keep him from humbling obedience. God had shown him that he had gotten caught up in the "busyness" of being a chaplain and in the vanity of psychology, all to the neglect of the Word of God. And so he had come to find out how to really dig into God's Word, to study it precept upon precept. He saw that a ministry without the Word of God as its pivotal point is not a life-giving or a life-changing ministry.

Our Shepherd said: "The words that I have spoken to you are spirit and are life" (John 6:63). "Man shall not live on bread alone, but on every word that proceeds out of the mouth of God" (Matthew 4:4). And thus our Shepherd's final earthly prayer was for His sheep, "Sanctify them [make them holy] in the truth; Your word is truth" (John 17:17).

When a person thinks he can live by bread alone, when he has been taken captive "through philosophy and empty deception, according to the tradition of men, according to the elementary principles of the world, rather than according to Christ" (Colossians 2:8), man is anything but holy. Man is all messed up.

Sometimes as people sit under the teaching of God's Word, they burst out sobbing. Suddenly confronted with how they have transgressed God's Holy Word, their hearts break in remorse. They have done those things they ought not to have done, and there is no health in them. They are riddled with the seeping sores of sin…immorality, incest, pornography, abortion, divorce (once, twice, more), wounded children, dominated husbands, neglected wives. They are governed by destructive tongues and hardened hearts that have to be broken with the hammer of God's Word.

O Beloved, are you wandering about, foraging, searching, unable to rest, getting all messed up

because you won't spend time feeding in the pastures
the Shepherd has prepared for you?

What will it take to make you get into His Word?

"Before I was afflicted, I went astray, but now I keep
Your word....May Your compassion come to me that I
may live, for Your law is my delight" (Psalm 119:67,77).

⌒

*The Bible is the Book that holds hearts up to
the light as if held against the sun.*

—WILLIAM A. QUAYLE

Lord is my shepherd, I shall not want. He makes me lie down in green pastures; He leads me

beside quiet waters. He restores my soul; He guides me in the paths of righteousness for His na

"When I Am Afraid"

After 15 years, suddenly it was back. It came after she had boarded the plane. "It was like something was going to happen, and I had no control over it. I wanted to run, to get away, but I was caught on the plane. Before I was saved, when fear would hit me, I would run...I would get out of the house or wherever I was."

But this time she could not run. The fear that came over my dear friend that day was not the fear of flying, but a sudden fear for her child whom she had left behind. However, because it happened on a plane, the fear was transferred to flying. What a problem this presented, for every week she had to fly to another state to teach a Bible class.

Have there been times, Beloved, when you have suddenly been struck by fear? What did you do?

Even though I walk through the valley of the shadow of death, I fear no evil, for You are with

Sheep have a tendency to run when frightened. A sudden noise or disturbance can cause panic in the sheepfold. And when fear strikes, the sheep take off frantically in every direction...often into danger.

There is only one cure for fear as far as sheep are concerned. And it was the only cure for my friend. When sheep are suddenly struck by fear, the shepherd senses it immediately and quietly moves among them, reassuring them of his presence. As soon as the sheep become aware that the shepherd is with them, the desire to run vanishes; fear has been replaced by trust. *The Lord is my Shepherd, I shall not want. He makes me to lie down*—to rest, not to panic.

My friend soon realized that this fear was a fiery dart from the enemy and that to run would only cause Satan great delight. She learned she must turn and gaze upon her Shepherd the moment fear struck. "When I am afraid, I will put my trust in You. In God, whose word I praise, in God I have put my trust; I shall not be afraid. What can mere man do to me?" (Psalm 56:3,4). And so she would be kept in perfect peace by keeping her mind stayed upon her Shepherd...she would trust in Him (Isaiah 26:3).

When fear begins to grip your heart, you must stop at that very moment and remember that fear is not

me; Your rod and Your staff, they comfort me. You prepare a table before me in the presenc

from God. The Lord is your Shepherd, and you shall not want.

God has not given us the spirit of timidity, but of power and of love and of discipline (or a sound mind) (2 Timothy 1:7). Therefore, when you find yourself the target of the enemy's fiery darts of fear, you must raise your shield of faith. With this spiritual armor you will be able to extinguish all of the flaming arrows of the evil one (Ephesians 6:16).

A sound mind is a mind under control…a disciplined mind that does not panic, does not lose touch with reality, does not give way to imagination, does not lose consciousness or fall into depression. When fear would catch you in its viselike grip, you must consciously rehearse the love of God and remember His sovereignty. Remember, whatever comes your way has to be filtered through God's sovereign fingers of love, and perfect love casts out every torment of fear (1 John 4:18).

Recognizing all of this, and knowing that fear comes from the father of lies—that thief who would kill and destroy—you must then appropriate that power which is given to you by God. Remember that God has not given you the spirit of fear…but of power.

enemies; You have anointed my head with oil; my cup overflows. Surely goodness and

How do you appropriate this power? First, you must recognize that one of the enemy's favorite weapons of warfare is fear. So look to your Shepherd-God. Submit to Him. Tell Him you are His; He can do anything with you that He wants. This really discombobulates the enemy! Then "resist the devil and he will flee from you" (James 4:7).

Periodically, a sudden dart of fear will still take aim at my friend. But now she does not panic. The moment fear strikes, she consciously recognizes its source. She says it is almost as if the enemy cries, "Here comes that fear again. You aren't going to be able to handle it. You are going to go into a panic."

"But," she says, "I know it is him, the father of lies, the destroyer of peace, and I do not entertain the thought for a moment. I simply refuse it and go on with whatever I was doing."

O Beloved…this is how you, too, must handle fear. Look to the Shepherd; He's there. He'll never leave you nor forsake you. You can boldly say, "The LORD is my helper, I will not be afraid" (Hebrews 13:5,6).

lovingkindness will follow me all the days of my life, and I will dwell in the house of the Lord for

Resting in His Pasture

Are you tense? Edgy? Discontented? Restless? Irritable? When sheep get this way, they cannot lie down. Rest is impossible! These are sure signs there is rivalry, so the shepherd looks for friction within his flock. People aren't the only ones who compete for status or go about asserting themselves. These attitudes are also common among sheep, and when they are, oh, how the tension builds!

Authority within the sheepfold is established by a butting order.[3] In Ezekiel 34:20-22, God says to His wayward people:

"Behold, I, even I, will judge between the fat sheep and the lean sheep. Because you push with side and with shoulder, and thrust at all the weak with your horns until you have scattered them abroad, there-fore, I will deliver My flock, and they will no longer be a prey; and I will judge between one sheep and another."

O Beloved, how it must hurt our Shepherd's heart to see us butt, shove, and push one another just so we can be recognized, elevated, or established in author-ity over others.

The Good Shepherd came not to be ministered unto, but to minister, "to give His life a ransom for many" (Matthew 20:28). Jesus, who is God, did not exalt Himself; instead, He made Himself a servant (Philippians 2:5-7). How can we help but take this form also?

Did He not tell us that to become great in the kingdom of God we must become servants?

Are you missing that life of rest which is yours as His child, the sheep of His pasture, because you are trying to assert yourself...or because others are butting you out of the way?

When you sit in church next Sunday, look around you at the flock. What is your attitude toward them? And what is your attitude toward other groups of Christians who seem to be more successful or as successful as your group? Is there jealousy in your heart, or a spirit of rivalry? If so, you will not be able to lie down in the green pastures your Shepherd has prepared for you. If you have been "butting," confess it in your prayer right now.

～

The object of love is to serve, not to win.

—WOODROW WILSON

Even though I walk through the valley of the shadow of death, I fear no evil, for You are with

me; Your rod and Your staff, they comfort me. You prepare a table before me in the presenc

Satisfied by Living Water

Sheep cannot live without water. Yet they can go for months without actually drinking. How? By absorbing the dew on the grass. This moisture can satisfy their need until their grazing takes them to streams, springs, or wells where they can drink deeply.

The secret is to catch the grass or vegetation while it is still wet, and to do this, the sheep must be up and about early in the morning, before the sun dries up that clean, pure dew! Thus, the shepherd will make sure his sheep are out and grazing early. Then, when the heat of the day comes, the sheep will have already satisfied their hunger and thirst and can retire to the shade of a tree and lie down to rest.[4]

This is just the way our Shepherd seeks to lead us to the Water of Life. He knows the heat of our day,

enemies; You have anointed my head with oil; my cup overflows. Surely goodness and

the pressures that come as things get hot and busy, and so He bids us arise in the early hours and come graze with Him:

"The Lord GOD has given Me the tongue of disciples, that I may know how to sustain the weary one with a word. He awakens Me morning by morning, He awakens My ear to listen as a disciple" (Isaiah 50:4).

Now, Beloved, there is no law that says you must meet with God every morning or He will not bless you. Please do not think that! What I am suggesting is that if you want to remain serene, confident, and able to cope, you need to drink of Jesus, the Fountain of Living Water. And it is easier to do this, in all probability, if you meet with your Shepherd before the distractions of the day pull you away.

Unless you are getting good Bible study at church or with a group in your community, it can be a long time between springs, streams, or wells. So you must be sustained by your daily dew. I have found that once my day starts, the heat is on. Then it is difficult to get pure, clean dew…and without it my tongue is thick with thirst and certainly is not the tongue of a disciple!

Why not try it faithfully for just *one* month and see if that morning dew doesn't make a difference? Will you?

Safety with the Shepherd

"He leads me beside quiet waters" (Psalm 23:2). Sheep are frightened by swiftly moving streams. If they fall into the water, they can easily be carried downstream by the current. Also, if they have not been shorn and are thick with coats of wool, they can easily become waterlogged and sink. Sheep and rapid water do not mix, and sheep know it! Whenever they have to cross water of any depth at all, they know there is only one safe place, and that is next to the shepherd.

For this reason, our Shepherd says to us: "Do not fear, for I have redeemed you; I have called you by name; you are Mine! When you pass through the waters, I will be with you; and through the rivers, they will not overflow you" (Isaiah 43:1,2).

O precious one, have you tried to cross the waters alone? Have you been swept away by some sudden, swift current of events? Are you being pulled under, absorbing your problems rather than casting them off? Are you weighed down in the waters of trouble? Are you overwhelmed? Do you fear for your sanity of mind? Do you feel that you might not make it, that you might drown? Sheep who do not stay close to the Shepherd often feel that way.

Draw near. Quiet yourself. Listen to His words. Remember that He has said, "I will never desert you, nor will I ever forsake you" (Hebrews 13:5).

The waters will not overflow you. They cannot overflow you when you are close to Him. When the three Hebrew children were thrown into the furnace of fire, they saw a fourth there, the Son of God (Daniel 3:25). When all deserted the apostle Paul, the Lord stood with him and strengthened him (2 Timothy 4:16,17).

God has never forsaken His sheep. Would He begin with you? Of course not!

Write out a prayer to your Shepherd. Tell Him about the waters you are crossing.

beside quiet waters. He restores my soul; He guides me in the paths of righteousness for His na

∼

When peace like a river
Attendeth my way;
When sorrows like sea billows roll;
Whatever my lot
Thou hast taught me to say
It is well; it is well with my soul.

—H.G. Spafford

Even though I walk through the valley of the shadow of death, I fear no evil, for You are with

me; Your rod and Your staff, they comfort me. You prepare a table before me in the presence

The Restorer of Your Soul

*H*e leads me beside quiet waters. He restores my soul" (Psalm 23:2,3). What does the psalmist mean when he says the Shepherd "restores my soul"? To understand that, we need to understand what happens when a sheep becomes "cast"—"cast down."

A cast sheep is one that has rolled onto its back and is unable to get up. Sometimes a sheep will lie down to rest; then, deciding to have a good stretch on its side, it will suddenly get off balance. It may get caught on uneven ground, or it may be heavy with fat or wool or with lamb. Suddenly its center of gravity shifts, and the poor thing finds itself on its back. As the sheep flails its legs frantically in the air, trying to right itself, gases begin to build up in the animal's stomach. As these gases build, circulation to its legs is cut off. On its back, unable to get up, the sheep is utterly cast down. [5]

If the day is sunny and hot, the sheep will only last a few hours. A cast sheep is also easy prey for all sorts of predators. The shepherd is the only hope for a cast sheep, and when he spots one, he wastes no time. He hurries to rescue—to restore—his sheep.

Have you ever felt so "down" that you wondered if you would ever get up? Maybe depression has settled around you like a morning fog so that you have forgotten what it was like to awaken to days of expectation, bright with clear blue skies and white cotton-puff clouds. Or perhaps you feel abandoned by God. You know God's Word says that He will not forsake you, but for some reason you feel He has.

If this describes you, it may be that you are "cast down."

Fear not, little sheep. The omniscient, omnipresent Lord is your Shepherd! If you are cast down and unable to get up, He knows where you are. He knows the enemy's predators are all around, seeking to devour you (1 Peter 5:8). Cry to Him. Let Him heal your "bleating." He will rescue you. He will restore your soul.

lovingkindness will follow me all the days of my life, and I will dwell in the house of the Lord fore

"The Lord sustains all who fall and raises up all who are bowed down" (Psalm 145:14).

Those, Beloved, are the words of your Shepherd.

～

Loving Shepherd of Thy sheep,
Keep Thy lamb, in safety keep;
Nothing can Thy power withstand,
None can pluck me from Thy hand.

—JANE E. LEESON

Lord is my shepherd, I shall not want. He makes me lie down in green pastures; He leads me

beside quiet waters. He restores my soul; He guides me in the paths of righteousness for His nar

Do You Need to Be Restored?

re you locked in a situation of despair? Have your tears been your food day and night? Have others said to you, "Where is your God?" (Psalm 42:3). Do you wonder why you are where you are or if you will ever change? Or if the depression will ever go away? If so, precious sheep, you are once more cast down and need to be restored.

Sheep usually become cast down for one of four reasons.

First, many sheep become cast while looking for a soft spot—a cozy, rounded hollow in the ground. They want it easy. But it is in these soft hollows that they are more apt to end up on their back.

People are much the same. People with time on their hands, or people with no outreach, or people

Even though I walk through the valley of the shadow of death, I fear no evil, for You are with

who tend to be preoccupied with their own problems are susceptible to depression. Because things are easy or soft, they have time to think, to focus on the negatives in their lives. And ofttimes it rolls them right over on their backs.

The *second* reason many sheep become cast is that they are fat. Overweight sheep are not only the quickest to become caught off-balance, but they are also the least productive and the least healthy. They simply have too much abundance.

How like us! Once we have it made, once we get fat with the over-abundances of life, we see little need to depend upon our Shepherd. Our "busyness," our preoccupation with getting ahead or with keeping up a certain lifestyle, lands us flat on our backs. We forget what it is like to walk in dependence upon our Shepherd, and so we are caught, fat and empty.

Let's stop and take a good, honest look at ourselves. Could we become cast sheep? Any sheep can...the largest, the strongest, the fattest, the healthiest.

Are you looking for an easy, soft life? Are you getting fat, living luxuriously on the things of the world? Are you entangling yourself in the affairs of this life rather than pleasing Him who has called you to be a soldier (2 Timothy 2:4)?

When a sheep has too much wool, its fleece becomes clogged with mud, sticks, burrs, ticks, and manure. The wool, laden with all of this, puts so much weight on the sheep that it just cannot get up. And that's the *third* reason a sheep can become cast down and need restoring.

If a sheep has become cast because of its wool, the shepherd knows that it is time to shear his sheep. This clogged fleece has to go! His sheep must be stripped down to keep from being cast down!

Not unlike us, Beloved. Did you know that God did not allow His priests who were ministering in the tabernacle to wear wool because wool was a picture of the self-life? We must all be careful of that self-life that can become clogged with sins and encumbrances that would so easily weigh us down. Every encumbrance and the sin which so easily entangles has got to be laid aside (Hebrews 12:1).

You would think the shepherd of such a sheep would just let it go. After all, it was the sheep who made such a repulsive mess of itself…just let it stay on its back. But this is impossible for the Great

enemies; You have anointed my head with oil; my cup overflows. Surely goodness and

Shepherd, who gave His very life for this sheep. He came to seek and to save the lost. And so when He finds that one, flat on its back, legs stiff and paralyzed, there is great rejoicing.

Tender words of loving rebuke, of admonition, and of instruction spill from the Shepherd's mouth as He reaches down to this sheep He knows so well. Turning it upon its side, the Shepherd massages its legs, restoring the circulation so that it can again walk at His side.

Finally, a ewe heavy with lambs can become cast. Sometimes, Beloved, those who are bearing the care of others or those burdened with a ministry can suddenly find themselves on their backs, weighted down...unable to get up on their feet. How vital it is that such a one walk continuously at the Shepherd's side, being careful to rest on solid ground, wary of hollows that would throw him or her off balance.

May we remember that He "will gently lead the nursing ewes" (Isaiah 40:11). And may we allow ourselves to be led.[6]

The Shepherd never drives His sheep. He always leads them.

lovingkindness will follow me all the days of my life, and I will dwell in the house of the Lord for

If You Go Astray

*A*ll of us like sheep have gone astray, each of us has turned to his own way" (Isaiah 53:6). "Before I was afflicted I went astray" (Psalm 119:67).

It is sad when dependent sheep try to live in an independent manner. Some sheep are just plain stubborn! They just don't want to stay with the flock. They want to graze where they want to graze. They don't want to follow the shepherd; they want the shepherd to follow them...or to at least be there should they need him. And need him they will if they keep wandering off. You see, sheep are so dumb that they can eat their way right off a cliff!

Lord is my shepherd, I shall not want. He makes me lie down in green pastures; He leads me

When a shepherd has a sheep with an independent streak, he often has to take radical action to keep the sheep from "self-destructing." The shepherd will break the sheep's leg. He'll catch that wandering, independent sheep, lay it down, and break its leg with a rock. But his purpose is not to hurt or cripple the sheep. For after breaking the sheep's leg, he tenderly binds it in a splint. Then he lifts the helpless creature to his bosom and enfolds it in his robe.

Brokenness has brought the sheep to the bosom of the shepherd. There it will feel the tender caresses of the shepherd. There it will feel the beat of the shepherd's heart. There it will hear the shepherd's every word. There it will be fed by the shepherd's hand. There…because of brokenness…the sheep will get to know the shepherd as it has never known him. Then, when the leg is mended, the sheep, having become accustomed to intimacy with its shepherd, will follow closely at his side.

"The LORD is near to the brokenhearted" (Psalm 34:18).

"The sacrifices of God are a broken spirit; a broken and a contrite heart, O God, You will not despise" (Psalm 51:17).

O Beloved, have you been prone to wander? Have you been broken? Can you not see the love of the Shepherd in that brokenness?

He has broken your independent spirit so that you might dwell near Him in safety. Do not be bitter; He moved in love with your highest good in mind. Will you not thank Him for breaking you?

⌒

O to grace how great a debtor
Daily I'm constrained to be!
Let Thy goodness, like a fetter,
Bind my wandering heart to Thee.
Prone to wander, Lord, I feel it,
Prone to leave the God I love;
Here's my heart, O take and seal it,
Seal it for Thy courts above.

—ROBERT ROBINSON

Even though I walk through the valley of the shadow of death, I fear no evil, for You are with

me; Your rod and Your staff, they comfort me. You prepare a table before me in the presenc

Live...for His Name's Sake

re you in a rut? Has life become a boring, meaningless existence? Do you feel that were you to die tomorrow, you would have lived a life that never really had any significant effect upon others? If you can answer yes to any of these questions, then it is time to follow the Shepherd who will lead you "in the paths of righteousness for His name's sake" (Psalm 23:3). For, Beloved, you were chosen by Him that you might go and bear fruit (John 15:16).

Sheep are creatures of habit. Left to themselves, they will graze the same ground over and over again until the land becomes wasteland and their paths erode into gullies. Ground overgrazed by sheep often becomes polluted with parasites and disease. This is why sheep so desperately need a shepherd. They must be managed; they must be led on to new pastures, to prepared tables of land where they can be properly fed.[7]

Our Shepherd has prepared abundant pastures for us. But, alas, how many prefer the contaminated ruts to the new and greener grazing grounds He would lead us to if we were only willing to follow.

If you are in a rut or feel that life is meaningless, let me ask you:

— When was the last time you diligently sought God's face in prayer, asking Him to reveal His will to you?

— When was the last time you prostrated yourself in prayer and said, "Use me, God, or I'll die! I must worship You by serving You"?

— When was the last time you took the opportunity to counsel a needy one, visit the sick or those abandoned in nursing homes, cook a meal for someone, babysit for a young mother? When was the last time you encouraged younger women to become better wives and mothers or counseled younger men to become better husbands and fathers, prepared yourself in God's Word, encouraged some fainthearted Christian, worked at being a better partner or a better parent or a better child, cared for the orphans and the widows, or shared the precious truths of His Word with others?

Are you being led in paths of righteousness for His name's sake, or are you living in the rut of self-centeredness?

Ask your Shepherd where He would lead you.

～

This is a sane, wholesome, practical working faith:
That it is a man's business to do the will of
God...that God himself takes care of the man,
and...that therefore man ought never
to be afraid of anything.

—GEORGE MACDONALD

Lord is my shepherd, I shall not want. He makes me lie down in green pastures; He leads me

beside quiet waters. He restores my soul; He guides me in the paths of righteousness for His na

Your Valleys...
Chosen for You

*E*very now and then it happens, and yesterday was such a day. It was unseasonably warm, bright, and exquisitely beautiful, and I couldn't bear to drive my car down the hill to our office. I had to walk. As I came down through the grass, I felt like doing a Julie Andrews...running, twirling, and singing, "The hills are alive with the sound of music." I couldn't thank my Father enough for the beauty and warmth of it all.

Yet every day cannot be sunny, and night must always follow day. If there are to be mountains, there must of necessity be valleys.

"Even though I walk through the valley of the shadow of death, I fear no evil," says the psalmist, "for You are with me" (Psalm 23:4).

It is at this point in the Twenty-third Psalm that the pronouns change…from "He" to "You." And with the change of pronouns comes a change in atmosphere. All of a sudden we become acutely aware of the intimacy of the two walking together. Why? Because they are in a valley of deep darkness. The light of the sun has been blocked out by a looming mountain.

The path that the Shepherd has *chosen* for His sheep passes through a valley. It is dark in the valley; shadows cast frightening images; wild winds and storms can whip down suddenly and violently from the mountain. Why come this way?

Why? Because in the valleys can be found more abundant sources of water, where the sheep can drink long and deep. Also, the valleys are the way to the mountaintop's luscious vegetation!

Jesus stood and cried out, "If anyone is thirsty, let him come to Me and drink. He who believes in Me, as the Scripture said, 'From his innermost being will flow rivers of living water'" (John 7:37,38).

Valleys are not meant to depress or to irritate you, Beloved. They are not there to make you tremble. Valleys are passageways that will bring you into hitherto unexperienced intimacy with your Shepherd.

me; Your rod and Your staff, they comfort me. You prepare a table before me in the presen

If you are in a valley…if the sun is shut out…do not fear, precious sheep. Your Shepherd, God's Son, is there with you. It is all in His plan. He has an eternal purpose. He doesn't intend evil, only good.

...lovingkindness will follow me all the days of my life, and I will dwell in the house of the Lord fore...

His Staff...
Your Comfort

S he had lived for ten years in a dark underground dungeon. Her only light came at mealtimes when she was provided with a candle. Although Louis XIV had condemned her to prison, Madame Guyon knew that, like Paul, she was the Lord's prisoner, not the king's. In her tenth year of imprisonment, she wrote these words:

> A little bird I am, shut from the fields of air;
> Yet in my cage I sit and sing to Him who placed
>   me there;
> Well pleased a prisoner to be,
> Because, my God, it pleases Thee.[8]

O Beloved, have you ever wondered how people can be imprisoned and still sing? Have they been

Lord is my shepherd, I shall not want. He makes me lie down in green pastures; He leads me

given an extra portion of God, of His grace? Do they have something we could never even dream of attaining?

Remember when we talked about walking through the valley of the shadow of death and fearing no evil because our Shepherd is with us? Well, I didn't finish the fourth verse, which goes on to say, "I fear no evil, for You are with me; Your rod and Your staff, they comfort me" (Psalm 23:4).

As the sheep pass through the valley, there's no fear, for they experience the comfort of His presence through the touch of His staff.

The shepherd's staff is the extension of the shepherd's hand. It is used to rescue sheep, to draw the sheep together, to restore lambs to their ewes, and to guide the sheep. And last, but most precious, the shepherd uses his staff to touch his sheep so that he can have intimate contact with them while he walks beside them and towers above them.

Isn't this just like the Holy Spirit? The Spirit is the staff of comfort and guidance, the extension between our Shepherd's hand and us.

Didn't Jesus promise, "I will not leave you as orphans; I will come to you" (John 14:18)?

beside quiet waters. He restores my soul; He guides me in the paths of righteousness for His nar

"I will ask the Father, and He will give you another Helper, that He may be with you forever" (John 14:16).

So remember, Beloved, wherever you are, no matter how dark the valley, His staff…His Spirit…is your Comforter.

∼

Helper

Comforter

Holy Spirit

Even though I walk through the valley of the shadow of death, I fear no evil, for You are with

me; Your rod and Your staff, they comfort me. You prepare a table before me in the presenc

His Rod...
Your Protection

hy do some Christians seem to have a much more intimate relationship with the Father? One of the major reasons, I believe, is that they have come to know the purpose and, thus, the power of their Shepherd's rod.

The shepherd's rod is an extension of his right arm, the arm of power and authority. And what is our power and authority? The Word of God! By it we live; by it we rule. The shepherd's rod, like God's Word, is a weapon of power and protection.

The shepherd uses his rod to examine his sheep. As the sheep pass under his rod, the shepherd examines each one intimately to determine its needs and to discover any hidden problems that might cause the creature to be weak or infirm.

enemies; You have anointed my head with oil; my cup overflows. Surely goodness and

"I will make you pass under the rod," says our Great Shepherd (Ezekiel 20:37). And so He watches over us, carefully examining us in the light of His Word, revealing any infirmities, and cleansing us with the water of the Word.

The shepherd also uses his rod as a weapon to ward off predators.

How intimate are you with your Shepherd's rod, Beloved? Do you know its power, authority, and protection against the attacks of the enemy? Do you know the cleansing and, thus, the protection that the Word of God brings? Are you examined by its authority daily?

Remember when I shared with you that I was having to deal with loneliness and feelings of rejection? That is like a valley of the shadow of death—death to what I want, what I would like to be true, but isn't. Remember the young man who had been so horribly abused by his parents? Remember the friends who are having to deal with a cancerous brain tumor? For all of us, even in the midst of such dark valleys, because we are the sheep of His pasture there is comfort, succor, and sustenance through the Word of God. His

Word meets our every need; it holds the answer to our every question.

Spend some time looking up the following verses: 2 Timothy 3:16,17; Hebrews 4:12; Ephesians 5:26; Ephesians 6:16,17. Next to each reference write down what you learn about the Word.

Let His rod comfort you, Beloved.

⟋

*Your word is a lamp to my feet
and a light to my path.*

—PSALM 119:105

beside quiet waters. He restores my soul; He guides me in the paths of righteousness for His nam

His Table...
Prepared for You

"You prepare a table before me in the presence of my enemies" (Psalm 23:5).

Through the years, many a range war has raged between cattlemen and sheepherders. Why? Because sheep can ruin the land. They will eat the very root of a plant, thus leaving the land barren. For this reason, sheep must be kept on the move.

Many times the shepherd will scout ahead to prepare a mesa for the sheep's grazing, carefully removing certain plants that can poison sheep. In addition to making sure there is adequate water, the shepherd also scouts out the area to discover any predators that occupy the land.

When I think of how the Shepherd prepares "a place of feeding" for His sheep, even in the midst of

Even though I walk through the valley of the shadow of death, I fear no evil, for You are with

their enemies, I cannot help but think of the story of John Sung.

John was a brilliant young Chinese man who came to America to study. While in seminary, he came under conviction from God that he was not truly saved. Because of this, he fell into a severe depression. The faculty of the school were greatly concerned and were debating what to do with John when his depression suddenly gave way to an unrestrained exuberance! Not realizing that the change in John was the result of his salvation, they committed him to a mental institution.

John tried to escape but failed. Dark thoughts of ending his life took form in his mind...until the Lord rebuked him.

"If you can endure this trial patiently for 193 days," God said, "you will have learned how to...walk the Calvary road of unswerving obedience." Little did John realize that his Shepherd had gone before and prepared a table for him in the presence of his enemies.

Seeing his ordeal in a new light, John moved under his Shepherd's rod. He devoted his waking hours to reading the Bible. He read it through 40 times, each time using a different scheme of study.[9]

As a result of this time shut up with God and His Word, John Sung was to become a brilliant flame for God in the Far East.

What table has God prepared for you, dear sheep? May you sit at it peacefully as you realize your Shepherd prepared it.

enemies; You have anointed my head with oil; my cup overflows. Surely goodness and

...ovingkindness will follow me all the days of my life, and I will dwell in the house of the Lord forever

Oil...for Your Irritations

Have you ever gotten a bug up your nose? I have! Don't ask me how! But you can be sure that neither of us planned it...neither me nor the bug! Somehow either that bug got off course or my sniff just had too much power to it. At any rate, I felt as though I had inhaled a Mexican jumping bean. The poor thing was darting back and forth, up and down, apparently panicked by my violent shaking, snorting, and blowing. (It was found dead in my handkerchief.)

When I read *A Shepherd Looks at Psalm 23*, I discovered just how much we have in common with sheep. Bugs up their noses drive them to distraction! They certainly can't rest in that condition!

Sheep can suffer greatly because of the nose fly. This insect seeks to deposit its eggs on the mucous membrane of the sheep's nose. There the eggs hatch into small, wormlike larvae that eventually work their way up the nose into the sheep's head. As these larvae burrow into the sheep's flesh, they cause a tremendous irritation which in turn causes the sheep to thrash and beat its head against anything it can find. A sheep can become so driven to distraction by the irritation that it will actually kill itself trying to get rid of the aggravation.[10]

As I learned this truth, I could not help but think of how men and women can be tormented by the thoughts that burrow their way into their flesh. The eggs of torment are laid by the enemy and hatch into repulsive, destructive worms that work their way into our minds. Thoughts of fear, rejection, bitterness, hatred, failure, incompetency, sensuality, despair, and greed and more plague God's sheep, tormenting them, even driving some to suicide.

But is this to be the fate of God's sheep? No! Just as there is an oil the shepherd can prepare to protect his sheep from nose flies and their destructive work, so our Shepherd has a way to keep His sheep from such torment. As the psalmist says, "You have anointed my head with oil" (Psalm 23:5).

Let me ask you a question, Beloved. Is there a bug tormenting you? What is it? Write it down. Then ask your Shepherd for His oil.

Oil...for Your Peace

*S*atan is the Christian's nose fly. His target is your mind. He wants to deposit thoughts in your mind which will hatch lies that will burrow their way into your flesh and drive you to distraction. Satan will do anything he can to destroy you, for "he was a murderer from the beginning...he is a liar and the father of lies" (John 8:44).

"I hate my little boy, but I don't know why. I know it's wrong. I try to love him, but I can't." The woman who said this had come to my friend for counseling.

As my friend shared the situation with me, she said, "There's only one thing I learned that might give us a clue to her problem. One day when she picked her little son up from the sitter's house, the sitter's neighbor commented that she hated screaming children. Ever since then this precious girl has been panicked about her child making a fuss in public."

enemies; You have anointed my head with oil; my cup overflows. Surely goodness and

As we prayed about the situation, both of us felt this was our clue from the Lord. Satan had planted a lie in that woman's head through the neighbor's comment. In light of this, my friend advised the dear mother to take captive the lie through warfare praying, resisting the enemy, and refusing his lies.

The woman prayed something like this: "O Father, I refuse this lie from the enemy. Satan, you are a liar and destroyer, and I will have nothing to do with you. I command you to depart with this lie. Father, You love my son just as he is. He is a gift from You. You designed him in my womb, and I love him and thank You for him."

Satan's destructive lie had caused her great torment, but she now knew where this hatred had come from—from the father of lies. Her Shepherd had anointed her head with His protective oil.

Beloved, has Satan deposited a lie in your mind? Do not despair. Instead, seek the Shepherd's oil, the healing balm of truth. Lies cannot survive when truth is applied to the wound day after day.

lovingkindness will follow me all the days of my life, and I will dwell in the house of the Lord fore

Oil...for Your Victory

During the season for nose flies or other pests that torment sheep, a good shepherd will prepare a special protective oil and smear it over the head and nostrils of each of his sheep.

So now, Beloved, since it is always the season for Satan's nose flies, let's get our heads duly treated with the Shepherd's oil. Remember, Satan's target is the mind, so God tells us in 2 Corinthians 10:5 that we are to destroy speculations and every lofty thing raised up against the knowledge of God. We are to take every thought captive to the obedience of Christ. This is the Shepherd's oil.

But how is it applied? By the raw, naked obedience of faith.

Lord is my shepherd, I shall not want. He makes me lie down in green pastures; He leads me

When a thought comes to your mind, before you grant it entrance you are to "Philippians 4:8" it: "Whatever is true, whatever is honorable, whatever is right, whatever is pure, whatever is lovely, whatever is of good repute, if there is any excellence and if anything worthy of praise, dwell on these things."

Every thought is to be frisked at the door of your mind before you let it in. Is it true? Honorable? Right? Pure? If the answer to *any* of the above is no, then you are not to think or dwell upon it.

But what do you do if the lying larvae have already dug into your flesh and set up their irritation? Then you need to perform some radical surgery. First, ask God to search your mind and reveal where the enemy has erected his stronghold. Then find the truth in the Word of God that refutes what Satan has said. When you find that truth, command Satan to leave you, and order the stronghold or fortress torn down by God's Holy Spirit. Tell God that you purposefully, willfully choose to believe His Word.

Ask the Lord Jesus Christ to stand there with you against the enemy's stronghold and, by your God's authority, destroy it, knowing that "the weapons of our warfare are not of the flesh, but divinely powerful for the destruction of fortresses" (2 Corinthians 10:4).

Then, in faith, praise God, for you are more than a conqueror through Him. Should the thought try to come back again, refuse it...over and over again... until it gets weary and flies away exhausted. Then, Beloved, your cup will overflow (Psalm 23:5)!

Whatever is true
Whatever is honorable
Whatever is right
Whatever is pure...

Even though I walk through the valley of the shadow of death, I fear no evil, for You are with

me; Your rod and Your staff, they comfort me. You prepare a table before me in the presen

Known...Loved...
by the Shepherd

Beloved, do you ever feel lost in the crowd...like you are not important or significant? You look at other Christians and feel that they are the superstars...the greats...the ones who are really being used by God. And then there is you.

Of course you would never let anyone know that you feel this way, but it would be kind of nice to hear your own name mentioned now and then. It would feel good, at least, to be recognized...at least just once. But, then, it will probably never happen, because you are not *important*...so who would remember your name?

O Beloved...*NO, NO, NO! You are wrong. You are precious. You are important. You are special. You are His sheep. Turn around and look. Goodness and lovingkindness are*

enemies; You have anointed my head with oil; my cup overflows. Surely goodness and

following you. You are so special that you will dwell in the house of the Lord forever. You are His...He has called you by your name. Oh, how I wish I could put my arms around you and tell you this truth in person.

"I am the good shepherd, and I know My own and My own know Me" (John 10:14). God knows you, precious one, by name (John 10:3). You are not just one of a flock, but an individual who is very precious to your Shepherd. You are so special to Him that if He had 99 other sheep and you were lost, He would know that you were the one missing. And He would not stop looking for you, calling you by name, until He had found you (Luke 15:3-6).

Your name is important to Him. To Him you are very significant...very precious. Don't ever forget it, Beloved.

Oh, you may not be known by multitudes, but what does that matter, for you are known to your Shepherd, the King of kings. And He is coming again to "receive you to Myself, that where I am, there you may be also" (John 14:3).

You will dwell in the house of the Lord forever (Psalm 23:6). And do you know what? You will never want because the Lord is your Shepherd.

Write a love note to your Shepherd. Thank Him for His tender care, and tell Him that you will follow wherever He leads.

∼

He leadeth me, O blessed thought!
O words with heavenly comfort fraught!
Whate'er I do, where'er I be
Still 'tis God's hand that leadeth me.

He leadeth me, He leadeth me,
By His own hand He leadeth me.
His faithful follower I would be
For by His hand He leadeth me.

—JOSEPH GILMORE

Notes

1. Bull, Geoffrey, *God Holds the Key* (Hodder, 1962).
2. Keller, W. Phillip, *A Shepherd Looks at Psalm 23* (Grand Rapids, MI: Zondervan, 1970), p. 23. Used by permission.
3. Ibid., p. 28
4. Ibid., p. 42.
5. Ibid., p. 51.
6. Ibid., pp. 57,58.
7. Ibid., p. 61.
8. Thompson, Phyllis, *Madam Guyon: Martyr of the Holy Spirit* (London: Hodder and Stoughton, 1986), p. 156.
9. Lyall, Leslie T., *John Sung: Flame for God in the Far East* (Chicago, IL: Moody Press, 1964), p. 42.
10. Keller, *A Shepherd Looks at Psalm 23*, p. 112.

beside quiet waters. He restores my soul; He guides me in the paths of righteousness for His na